When I Am Gloomy
当我忧郁时

Sam Sagolski
Illustrated by Daria Smyslova

www.kidkiddos.com
Copyright ©2025 by KidKiddos Books Ltd.
support@kidkiddos.com

All rights reserved. No part of this book may be reproduced in any form or by any electronic or mechanical means, including information storage and retrieval systems, without written permission from the publisher, except in the case of a reviewer, who may quote brief passages embodied in critical articles or in a review.
First edition, 2025

Translated from English by Yusin Hu
胡郁欣译自英语

Library and Archives Canada Cataloguing in Publication
When I Am Gloomy (English Simplified Chinese Bilingual edition)/Shelley Admont
ISBN: 978-1-0497-0123-3 paperback
ISBN: 978-1-0497-0124-0 hardcover
ISBN: 978-1-0497-0125-7 eBook

Please note that the English and Simplified Chinese versions of the story have been written to be as close as possible. However, in some cases they differ in order to accommodate nuances and fluidity of each language.

One cloudy morning, I woke up feeling gloomy.

在一个多云的早晨,我起床便觉得很忧郁。

I got out of bed, wrapped myself in my favorite blanket, and walked into the living room.

我离开我的床铺,把自己包裹在我最爱的毯子里,然后走进客厅。

"Mommy!" I called. "I'm in a bad mood."
"妈咪!"我喊道。"我心情很不好。"

Mom looked up from her book. "Bad? Why do you say that, darling?" she asked.
妈妈从她的书中抬起头来。"很不好?你为什么这么说啊,亲爱的?"她问道。

"Look at my face!" I said, pointing to my furrowed brows. Mom smiled gently.
"看我的脸!"我说,一边指着我皱起的眉头。妈妈温柔地笑了。

"I don't have a happy face today," I mumbled. "Do you still love me when I'm gloomy?"
"我今天没有快乐的表情,"我咕哝着。"当我忧郁的时候,你依然会爱我吗?"

"Of course I do," Mom said. "When you're gloomy, I want to be close to you, give you a big hug, and cheer you up."

"我当然会,"妈妈说。"当你忧郁的时候,我想要陪在你身旁,给你一个大大的拥抱,并让你振作起来。"

That made me feel a little better, but only for a second, because then I started thinking about all my other moods.

那让我觉得好一些了，但只维持了一秒钟，因为我接着开始思考我其他不同的心情。

"So… do you still love me when I'm angry?"
"所以…我生气的时候你也还会爱我吗?"

Mom smiled again. "Of course I do!"
妈妈又笑了。"我当然会!"

"Are you sure?" I asked, crossing my arms.
"你确定吗?"我问道,交叉着双臂。

"Even when you're mad, I'm still your mom. And I love you just the same."

"即使你很生气,我依然是你的妈妈。而且我爱你一如既往。"

I took a big breath. "What about when I'm shy?" I whispered.

我深吸了一口气。"那当我觉得很害羞的时候呢？"我悄声地说。

"I love you when you're shy too," she said. "Remember when you hid behind me and didn't want to talk to the new neighbor?"

"你害羞的时候我也爱你，"她说。"还记得你躲在我身后，不想和新邻居说话的时候吗？"

I nodded. I remembered it well.

我点点头，我记得很清楚。

"And then you said hello and made a new friend. I was so proud of you."

"然后你说了你好,并交到了一个新朋友。我真为你骄傲。"

"Do you still love me when I ask too many questions?" I continued.

"当我问太多问题的时候你还会爱我吗？"我继续道。

"When you ask a lot of questions, like now, I get to watch you learn new things that make you smarter and stronger every day," Mom answered. "And yes, I still love you."

"当你问很多问题的时候，比如现在，我能看到你在学习新的事物，这让你每天都变得更聪明、更强壮，"妈妈回答说。"而且是的，我依然爱你。"

"What if I don't feel like talking at all?" I continued asking.
"那如果是我完全不想讲话的时候呢?"我继续问道。

"Come here," she said. I climbed into her lap and rested my head on her shoulder.
"过来这里,"她说。我爬到她的腿上,把我的头放在她的肩膀上。

"When you don't feel like talking and just want to be quiet, you start using your imagination. I love seeing what you create," Mom answered.

"当你不想说话,只想安安静静的时候,你会开始运用自己的想象力。我非常喜欢看你的创作,"妈妈回答道。

Then she whispered in my ear, "I love you when you're quiet too."

然后她在我耳边轻声说,"你安静的时候我也爱你。"

"But do you still love me when I'm afraid?" I asked.
"但是当我害怕的时候,你还爱我吗?"我问。

"Always," said Mom. "When you're scared, I help you check that there are no monsters under the bed or in the closet."
"永远不变,"妈妈说。"当你害怕的时候,我会帮你检查床底下或衣橱里有没有怪物。"

She kissed me on the forehead. "You are so brave, my sweetheart."

她亲了亲我的额头。"你真勇敢,我的甜心。"

"And when you're tired," she added softly, "I cover you with your blanket, bring you your teddy bear, and sing you our special song."

"然后当你累了的时候,"她温柔地补充说,"我会给你盖上毯子,拿来你的泰迪熊,再给你唱我们那首特别的歌。"

"What if I have too much energy?" I asked, jumping to my feet.

"那如果是我太有活力的话呢？"我问，一边跳起来。

She laughed. "When you're full of energy, we go biking, skip rope, or run around outside together. I love doing all those things with you!"

她笑了。"当你精力充沛的时候，我们一起去骑自行车、跳绳或在外面跑来跑去。我非常喜欢和你一起做这些事！"

"But do you love me when I don't want to eat broccoli?" I stuck out my tongue.

"但是当我不想吃西兰花的时候,你爱我吗?"我吐了吐舌头。

Mom chuckled. "Like that time you slipped your broccoli to Max? He liked it a lot."

妈妈咯咯地笑了。"就像那次你偷偷把西兰花给马克斯那样?他很喜欢呢。"

"You saw that?" I asked.
"你看到了?"我问。

"Of course I did. And I still love you, even then."
"我当然看到了。而即使如此,我依然爱你。"

I thought for a moment, then asked one last question:

我想了一会儿,然后问了最后一个问题:

"Mommy, if you love me when I'm gloomy or mad… do you still love me when I'm happy?"

"妈咪,如果我忧郁或生气时你都爱我…那当我开心时你还会爱我吗?"

"Oh, sweetheart," she said, hugging me again, "when you're happy, I'm happy too."

"哦,甜心,"她说着,又抱了我一下,"当你开心的时候,我也会很快乐。"

She kissed me on the forehead and added, "I love you when you're happy just as much as I love you when you're sad, or mad, or shy, or tired."

她亲了亲我的额头,又说道:"你开心的时候我爱你,就像你伤心、生气、害羞或疲倦时我同样爱你。"

I snuggled close and smiled. "So… you love me all the time?" I asked.

我依偎着靠近,然后笑了。"所以…你一直都爱我?"我问。

"All the time," she said. "Every mood, every day, I love you always."

"一直都是,"她说。"每一种心情,每一天,我都永远爱你。"

As she spoke, I started feeling something warm in my heart.

她说这些话的时候，我开始觉得心里有东西暖暖的。

I looked outside and saw the clouds floating away. The sky was turning blue, and the sun came out.

我往外一看，看见云朵正在飘走。天空开始变得蔚蓝，然后太阳出来了。

It looked like it was going to be a beautiful day after all.

今天看起来会是很美好的一天。

www.ingramcontent.com/pod-product-compliance
Lightning Source LLC
LaVergne TN
LVHW072008060526
838200LV00010B/299